Dinosaur Detectives
Search for the Facts...

Archaeopteryx
and Other
Flying Reptiles

Tracey Kelly

BROWN BEAR BOOKS

Published by Brown Bear Books Ltd
4877 N. Circulo Bujia
Tucson, AZ 85718
USA

and

Leroy House
436 Essex Rd
London N1 3QP
UK

© 2018 Brown Bear Books Ltd

ISBN 978-1-78121-408-4

Library of Congress Cataloging-in-Publication Data available on request

Text: Tracey Kelly
Designer: John Woolford
Design Manager: Keith Davis
Editorial Director: Lindsey Lowe
Children's Publisher: Anne O'Daly
Picture Manager: Sophie Mortimer

Picture Credits
Shutterstock: Mikhail SH 4.

Brown Bear Books has made every attempt to contact the copyright holder.
If you have any information please contact: licensing@brownbearbooks.co.uk

Manufactured in the United States of America

CPSIA compliance information: Batch#AG/5609

Websites
The website addresses in this book were valid at the time of going to press. However, it is possible that contents or addresses may change following publication of this book. No responsibility for any such changes can be accepted by the author or the publisher. Readers should be supervised when they access the Internet.

Contents

How Do We Know about Dinosaurs?

Scientists are like detectives.

They look at dinosaur fossils.

Fossils tell us where dinosaurs lived.

They tell us how big they were.

This is an *Archaeopteryx* fossil. The first fossil was a feather. It was found in some rocks in Germany. Only 12 *Archaeopteryx* fossils have been found.

How to Use This Book

This tells you what the animal ate.

🌿 Plant-eater

🦕 Meat-eater

This tells you when the animal lived.

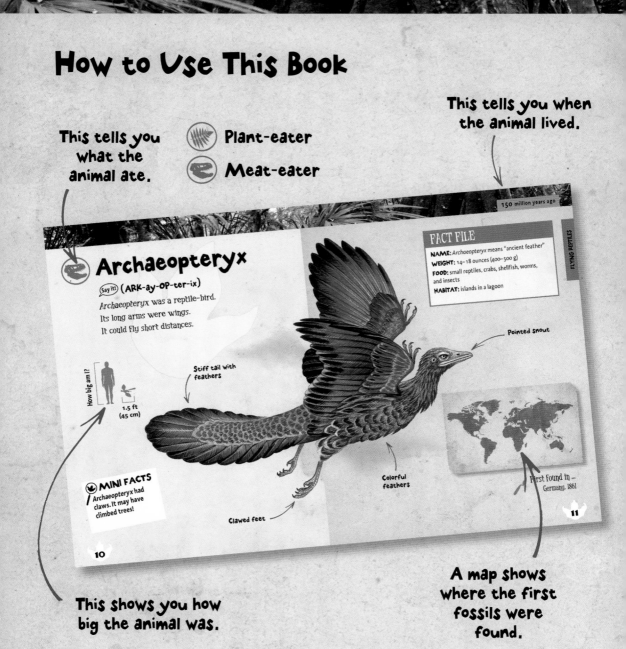

150 million years ago

FLYING REPTILES

Archaeopteryx

(Say it!) (ARK-ay-OP-ter-ix)

Archaeopteryx was a reptile-bird.
Its long arms were wings.
It could fly short distances.

How big am I?

1.5 ft
(45 cm)

Stiff tail with feathers

FACT FILE

NAME: *Archaeopteryx* means "ancient feather"
WEIGHT: 14–18 ounces (400–500 g)
FOOD: small reptiles, crabs, shellfish, worms, and insects
HABITAT: islands in a lagoon

Pointed snout

First found in ...
Germany, 1861

Colorful feathers

Clawed feet

⚘ MINI FACTS
Archaeopteryx had claws. It may have climbed trees!

10

11

This shows you how big the animal was.

A map shows where the first fossils were found.

Read on to become a dinosaur detective!

Flying Reptiles

Pterosaurs (TEH-row-sores)
were flying reptiles.
They lived 220 million years ago.
Pterosaurs were not dinosaurs.
But they lived at the same time.

Anurognathus

Say it! (ann-YOOR-rog-NAY-thus)

Anurognathus had a small tail and body.
It had leathery wings. It could change
direction quickly.

Sharp teeth for
grabbing prey

MINI FACTS

Scientists have
only found one
Anurognathus
skeleton.

How big am I?

20 in (50 cm) wingspan

FACT FILE

NAME: *Anurognathus* means "tailless jaw"
LENGTH: up to 3.5 inches (9 cm)
WEIGHT: 1½ ounces (40 g)
FOOD: insects
HABITAT: forests near shallow lagoons

Short fingers

Light wings

Toes with claws

First found in ...
Germany, before 1922

Archaeopteryx

Say it! (ARK-ay-OP-ter-ix)

Archaeopteryx was a reptile–bird.
Its long arms were wings.
It could fly short distances.

How big am I?

1.5 ft
(45 cm)

Stiff tail with feathers

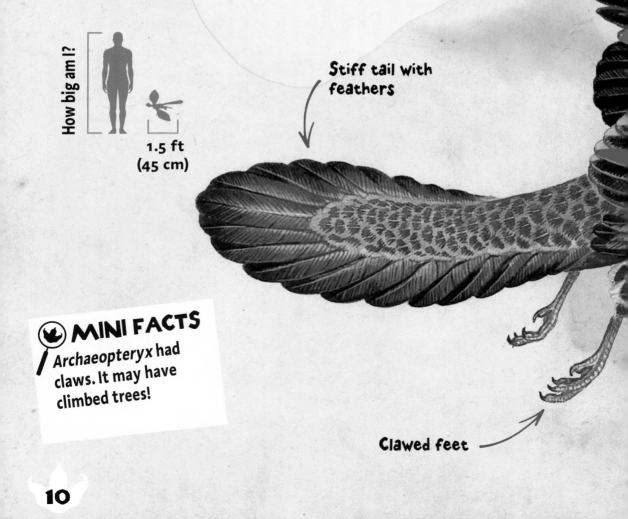

MINI FACTS
Archaeopteryx had claws. It may have climbed trees!

Clawed feet

FACT FILE

NAME: *Archaeopteryx* means "ancient feather"

WEIGHT: 14–18 ounces (400–500 g)

FOOD: small reptiles, crabs, shellfish, worms, and insects

HABITAT: islands in a lagoon

Pointed snout

Colorful feathers

First found in ...
Germany, 1861

11

Dimorphodon

Say it! (dye-MORF-oh-DON)

Dimorphodon was a flying pterosaur.
It had a huge head. Its front teeth were big.
They stuck out of its beak.

Claws used for grasping

How big am I?

4.5 ft (1.4 m)
wingspan

**Long front teeth
and tiny back teeth**

MINI FACTS
Dimorphodon's head
was half the length
of its body!

FACT FILE

NAME: *Dimorphodon* means "two-form tooth"

LENGTH: up to 3 feet (1 m)

FOOD: insects and small lizards

HABITAT: near coasts

Long wings

Wings made of skin

First found in ...
England, 1828

13

Eudimorphodon

Say it! **(you-dye-MORF-oh-DON)**

Eudimorphodon had a long beak.
It swooped low over the water.
Its sharp teeth snapped up fish.

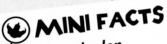

MINI FACTS

Eudimorphodon had about 55 teeth in each jaw.

Long beak to catch prey

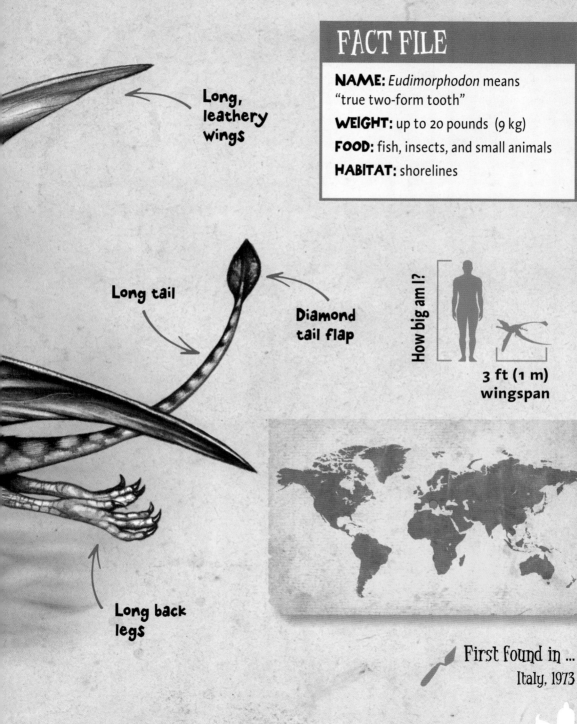

Long, leathery wings

FACT FILE

NAME: *Eudimorphodon* means "true two-form tooth"

WEIGHT: up to 20 pounds (9 kg)

FOOD: fish, insects, and small animals

HABITAT: shorelines

Long tail

Diamond tail flap

How big am I?

3 ft (1 m) wingspan

Long back legs

First found in ...
Italy, 1973

15

Kuehneosuchus

Say it! (KOON-ee-oh-SOO-chus)

Kuehneosuchus was a small lizard. It had long wing flaps. It could glide from trees.

How big am I?

Length 28 in
(71 cm)

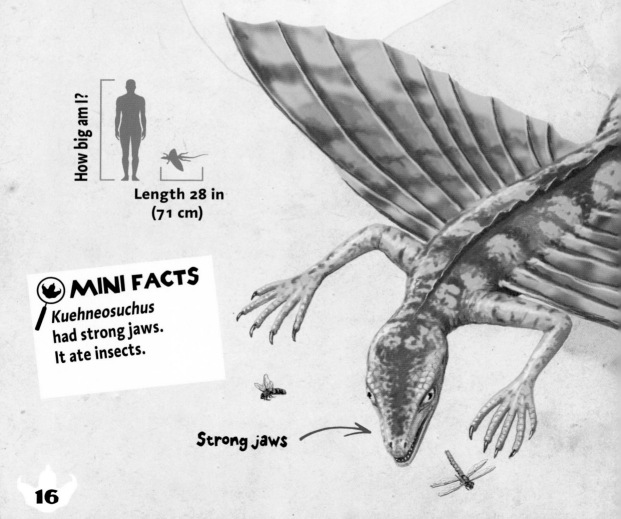

🐾 **MINI FACTS**

Kuehneosuchus had strong jaws. It ate insects.

Strong jaws

Long back legs
for running

FACT FILE

NAME: *Kuehneosuchus* means
"Keuhne's crocodile"

WINGSPAN: up to 16 inches (40 cm)

FOOD: insects

HABITAT: forests

First found in ...
England, 1962

Wing flaps

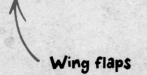

Pterodactylus

Say it! (TARE-oh-DAK-till-us)

Pterodactylus was a small pterosaur.
Its mouth was full of sharp teeth.
It hunted insects and fish.

Mouth had 90 teeth

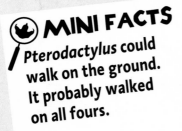

🐾 **MINI FACTS**

Pterodactylus could walk on the ground. It probably walked on all fours.

Long wings

How big am I?

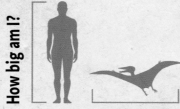

3 ft (1 m)
wingspan

Long wing fingers

Wing tip helped
to steer

FACT FILE

NAME: *Pterodactylus* means
"winged finger"

WEIGHT: about 10 pounds (4.5 kg)

FOOD: insects, fish, shellfish,
and small lizards

HABITAT: shores and rivers

Back legs
had claws

First found in ...
Germany, 1767–1784

19

Rhamphorhynchus

Say it! (RAM-for-RIN-kus)

Rhamphorhynchus had narrow wings.

It had a very long tail.

This made it a strong flier.

Spiky teeth

Wing fingers

How big am I?

6 ft (1.8 m)
wingspan

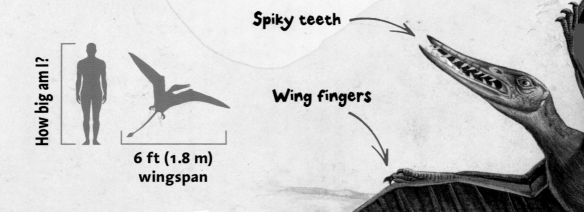

MINI FACTS
Rhamphorhynchus nested in big groups.

FACT FILE

NAME: *Rhamphorhynchus* means "beaked snout"

WEIGHT: about 7 pounds (3 kg)

FOOD: fish and insects

HABITAT: islands and shorelines

Leathery wing skin

Short back legs

First found in ...
Germany, named in 1846

Diamond-shaped tail

21

Dinosaur Quiz

Test your dinosaur detective skills!
Can you answer these questions?
Look in the book for clues.
The answers are on page 24.

2 What did this pterosaur eat?

1 Which pterosaur had two types of teeth?

3 Which reptile could glide from trees?

4 Which pterosaur probably walked on all fours?

Glossary

fossil
Part of an animal or plant in rock.
The animal or plant lived in ancient times.

habitat
The kind of place where an animal usually lives.

lagoon
A shallow pool near an ocean.

meat-eater
An animal that eats
mostly meat.

pterosaur
A flying reptile with
wings and a long
wing finger.

wing finger
The fourth finger
on a pterosaur.
It held up a wing.

Find out More

Books

The Big Book of Dinosaurs, DK Editors (DK Children, 2015)

National Geographic Kids Dinos Sticker Activity Book, National Geographic Kids Editors (National Geographic, 2014)

Websites

discoverykids.com/category/dinosaurs

www.kidsdinos.com/flying-reptiles

www.kids-dinosaurs.com/flying-dinosaurs.html

Index

Quiz Answers: 1. *Dimorphodon.* It had long front teeth and tiny back teeth.
2. *Anurognathus* ate insects. **3.** *Kuehneosuchus* could glide from trees.
4. *Pterodactylus.*